Copyright © 2023 by Lori Nakamura

All rights reserved.

No portion of this book may be reproduced in any form without written permission from the publisher or author, except as permitted by U.S. copyright law.

ISBN: 9798393260989

For our parents, who gave us so much.
Thank you for your sacrifices, love, and unwavering support.

-Lori & Leah

Pamilya

By Lori Nakamura
Illustrated by Leah Abucayan

I lived in a quaint house cozy and small,
with the people that I loved most of all,
Ate, Kuya, Mom and Dad,
Our years in that house were the best we had.

Our home was a place that was warm and inviting,
A giant spoon and fork on the wall was a regular sighting,
A reminder of the blessings of food and good health.
We prayed that Santo Niño would provide us with wealth.
The aroma of home-cooked Filipino cuisine,
Filled the air since my mom was a cooking machine.

She made the best pandesal, lumpia, and pancit.
Her food was made with love. There was no denying it.
She cared for us all and made breakfast, lunch, and dinner.
While my dad worked long hours as our family's breadwinner.
A traditional setup some would say,
But it worked for our family's day-to-day.
Ate and Kuya helped with the chores.
My job was the dishes and sweeping the floors.
We all worked together to keep the house clean,
Not one speck of dust could ever be seen.

It was most important to do well in school.
We had to get good grades because that was the rule.
We always worked hard and finished our work.
Good grades meant a reward, which was always a perk.

When reports cards came home and displayed our straight A's,
We earned some money and a trip to the arcade.
Our house was full of laughter. We were all so close knit.
And I would never ever trade the world for it.

Our family was like any other...or so I thought.
But others made me feel like perhaps we were not.
My parents had accents and spoke Tagalog at home.
We had mannerisms and traditions that to most were unknown.

There were not many like us in our small little town.
My skin was a different, unique shade of brown.
I had almond-shaped eyes and a rounder shaped nose,
My hair was as black as the darkest of crows.

It wasn't always easy being different at school.
Sometimes I was the center of ridicule.
My lunch looked strange and my name sounded funny.
My clothes were plain. We didn't have lots of money.

At times all I wanted was just to fit in,
To be like the rest,
To be in someone else's skin.
But then I realized how sad that must be,
To deny all the things that makes me...well, ME.

A photo of our family hung proud on the wall.
Beautiful brown smiling faces,
Five of us in all.
They are my pamilya, my anchor, my heart.
They'll always be there and have been from the start.

My parents worked hard and raised us well.
They always had stories from their hometown to tell.
I began to understand as I learned of their journey
The sacrifices they made for my ate, kuya, and me,
To give us the life that they never had,
Watching us succeed brought pride to Mom and Dad.

Before we were born my parents moved away,
From their country of birth where their family still stays.
The Philippine islands was the place they called home,
Suddenly they were in a new country alone.

No friends and no family, no familiar faces,
They came to a place full of all different races.
New people to meet, different cultures to know,
It was all so exciting, but still new to them though.

They sometimes felt lost and a little out of place,
But they took each challenge with smiles and grace.
They knew if they worked hard and also worked well,
One day they would have good news to tell.

This new place had opportunities and jobs that they'd need,
To provide for their family was what they agreed.

They missed all the people that they left behind,
But a new way of life is what they came to find.

And find it they did even with bumps in the road,
They persevered,
Found success,
It was their persistence that showed.
They overcame milestones both big and small.
They proved to us you can do anything at all.

Their idea of success revolved around the family.
To provide meant more than being rich financially.
They taught us to love and be kind most of all.
To be proud of who we are and to always stand tall.

My Filipino roots stretch even deeper than a tree,
Though I've never seen the Philippines, it is a part of me.
I know my family's history keeps me grounded to the floor.
The ones I love the most and who I am make up my core.

The outer part of me that you can see with just your eyes,
Make up my leaves and branches that reach upward toward the sky.
I'm proud of how I look and who I am and where I'm from.
All these things will help me be the man I will become.

I've learned that being different isn't something that is bad.
It can start a conversation that we all know must be had,
About how we're all just people in this world that we live in.
We must accept each other regardless of our melanin.

Our story is just one of so many, many more.
Everyone has a story of their family that came before.
If you open up your mind and try to learn from others too,
You'll find that we have more in common than you ever knew.

Now it's your turn. Draw your family

Write or Draw what makes you...**YOU**

About the Author and Illustrator

Lori Nakamura and **Leah Abucayan** are sisters who are first-generation Filipino-Americans. Growing up, they rarely saw anyone who looked like them in books or the media. Their goal was to tell a story that was uniquely Filipino, but still relatable to people of various backgrounds. It was important to them to create a book that honored their culture and family in a fun and meaningful way. Their hope is that this new generation of young readers will understand the impact of representation in books and know that their voices and stories are significant.

Follow them on Instagram @lorinakamura_author @hellaleah

This is their second book collaboration. Their first book, **Love Is More Contagious**, *was released in 2021 to help children dealing with the experience of quarantine during the COVID-19 pandemic.*

Lori lives in Granite Bay, California with her husband and two little girls. She has a degree in human development and a background in the performing arts. Today, she keeps busy teaching dance and fitness classes, making sourdough bread, driving her kids around to activities, and doing all the other things supermoms do, all while writing down ideas for her next book.

Leah lives in Atlanta, Georgia with her husband and her dog, Pepè. She received her education in graphic design at the Academy of Art in San Francisco. Currently, she works as a graphic designer for CNN and is also an accomplished muralist and duct tape artist. She spends her days tending to her plant babies, working out, playing with her dog, and taking on various commissioned art projects.

Made in the USA
Las Vegas, NV
18 October 2024